The Perfect HOME

Celebrity Designer Collections

by Joseph Carroll

Concept and Design by
Dianne Daly Barham

Table of

ISBN 0-9615307-0-7
First Edition

Copyright 2002 Furniture/Today
Reed Business Information
A Division of Reed Elsevier, Inc.

Contents

To Understand Another's Vision, You Must Be Able To Look Through Their Window

For more than 25 years, Bob Timberlake has made his living as a professional artist, painting the landscapes, people and everyday objects of his rural North Carolina home. In 1990 Timberlake awakened us to the joys of casual, comfortable living ... with style. The World of Bob Timberlake is defined by its warmth, comfort, and appeal to a wide variety of settings.

Bob Timberlake®

Bob Timberlake teamed up with Lexington Furniture in 1990 with a collection called *The World of Bob Timberlake*®. It changed the way we thought about furniture. No longer were we just buying another matched set of brown items, we were sharing the personality of a North Carolina artist who had a particular aesthetic sensibility. The public has enthusiastically responded to Bob's furniture because it has "personality" ... that we can trust and identify with.

Much of the success of the *Bob Timberlake Brand* can be attributed to the genuineness of Bob Timberlake himself and to the authenticity of his own lifestyle.

Bob is a strong believer in Heritage and Family. His father worked in a furniture store his grandfather started in the early 1900's. He enjoyed the relationships he had with his customers. He viewed their visits more like family gatherings or reunions. From his father, Bob learned that the best salesmen in the world were in love with what they were selling. Bob's licensees today include producers of home accessories, outdoor

First Light

furniture, apparel, clocks, home plans, home textiles, dinnerware, lighting, mirrors, paints & stains, rugs, throws and pillows and wallcoverings. He is still motivated by the philosophy that the whole idea of what he does is to bring joy and happiness into people's lives.

The Timberlake collections bring a relaxed sophistication to home furnishings. They take a casual approach to formal design ... comfortable and a bit eclectic. The 'Lodge' atmosphere Bob creates invites us to put our feet up, relax, and breath a little slower. You can almost smell the musty scent of wood smoke.

Big On Comfort

Bob Timberlake has a lifelong love of wood, furniture and nature. He will tell you that his feelings of Heritage and Family are the biggest, single, deep-rooted things that affect everything in his life, furniture included. "It separates our 'stuff' from others who don't have real and true feelings behind it – a real person and a true love of all that we do."

"I've been collecting things ever since I could bend over to pick up a pretty stone,"
Timberlake recalls. "First it was seashells and arrowheads; now it's folk art and
just about any other artifact of early life. These things hold so many stories about
the people who used them."

Bob Timberlake

Short Stories I

Make up your own short stories with rooms that encourage you to dress comfortably, watch a sunset or pull up to a fire with a good novel. Play a few hands of gin rummy … take time to recall memories or create new ones.

Decorating

Elegance Without The Fuss

Timberlake's designs were inspired by the simple, practical furnishings of his ancestors from the British Isles who crossed oceans, rivers and mountains to settle – among other places – in the Piedmont and mountains of North Carolina. Adventurous and adaptable, they built upon the traditions and skills they brought from home to meet the challenges of their new land.

Blueberries

Nature and texture have a major influence on Bob's painting. Charles Kuralt wrote, "The seasons are not merely a matter of solstice and equinox, but of the heat of the sun, the gathering of clouds, the rain of bright leaves on the cooling earth, the coming of storms and the still, chill night, and then the miracle of crocuses and jonquils breaking through the dried crystals of the last snowfall."

It's the small knots and other natural characteristics that make each wood piece unique and allow it to 'speak'. There are collector's tables to place your favorite collections right where you can see them. The dining room table expands to fit all the "kin" you can gather 'round for Thanksgiving dinner. Fabrics for the sofas and chairs have been selected for their warm and natural images. The deep, comfortable seating makes you feel like big, warm arms are wrapped around you … an environment that is both welcoming and personal.

"Home is at the heart of everything I have to share, as it always has been at the center of my life. At the heart of home, of course, is family. Home and family have made my life meaningful and worthwhile; they are at the core of everything I stand for."

Bob Timberlake

Memory Makir

Bob designs his furniture with friends and family in mind. A chair perfectly sized for granddad and his grandchildren or a sofa just the right size for a family snapshot create an inviting milieu for your own personal memories.

The Bob Timberlake Lodge Look evokes a simpler, more rugged time. It captures the elements of the outdoors we like to remember … the sound of rain on the roof, the smell of burning leaves in the fall, the crackle of a winter fire, or a hike through the country. Bob calls it 'bringing the outdoors in.'

Timberlake's furniture has come to symbolize a simpler, slower way of life. The increasingly hectic pace of life today gives us the desire to slow down. The Lodge Look relaxes. It allows our senses to be soothed in the comforts of our own home.

Relaxing Refreshing Retreats

The Lodge lifestyle offers a sense of both freedom and privacy. You continue to enjoy the textures, shapes and scents that you left outside. Among the textural accents are forged-look wrought iron, pottery, leather, rope, twigs and patchwork copper panels. Like a lodge itself, there's nothing fancy about the furniture. It's built for comfort and durability.

Zinnias

We share a recollection of a day when people did not move so much or so fast, when families and neighbors meant more, and money somewhat less. We still appreciate the surprises we can find in our own backyard.

Bob Timberlake's furniture is a fitting tribute to the woodworkers and craftspeople who inspire his art … the people he is often found with sharing a fishing tale in his hometown diner in Lexington, North Carolina.

Gracefully crafted pieces of cherry, oak, spruce or an aged paint finish reflect the character of the artist himself … honest, authentic and hospitable. For Bob, it's all about a love of heritage, home and family.

"Do I have a favorite piece of furniture? I'm afraid I don't," says Bob. "They're all special or we wouldn't have made them. I don't have a special favorite painting either – they're all special for different reasons."

Mix an antique or family hand-me-down with Timberlake's collection and it feels right at home. You also claim a personal ownership to the decorating scheme.

Where Your Heart

"*Whether it is through painting, designing a braided rug, or now, through my furniture collections, what always matters to me are the values of family, heritage, attention to detail and pride in a job well done.*"

Bob Timberlake

Jessica McClintock owns and operates her world famous design house in San Francisco. She is probably best known for the fashions she has designed for proms, graduations, weddings and special occasions as well as her line of women's fragrances. She is the recipient of numerous industry awards and has been consistently named among Working Women's Top 50 Woman Business Owners since 1994. The key to Jessica's success is her timeless and classic style.

Jessica McClintock

In 2000, American Drew, a La-Z-Boy company, introduced the Jessica McClintock Home Collection. American Drew agreed with Jessica's design philosophy that since most people collect memorable items during their lifetime, their homes should reflect their lives. Their home should represent and define the joy and peacefulness of their surroundings. Jessica's own preference is for homes that have fantasy and romance: "I feel every room in a house should be like a jewel box. I especially like beautiful moldings, glazes on walls, faux paintings in soft, delicate pastels and beautiful floors. I love furniture that has artistic ornamentation inspired by our historical past. I especially love Eighteenth Century antiques. I love the patina of old pieces and the beauty of timeless design."

If you share Jessica's love for the romantic settings of the old homes found in Merchant Ivory movies such as *A Room With a View* and *Wings of a Dove*, you doubtless love their timeless furnishings … the soft colors and antique finishing. We enjoy the drama of these settings that is reminiscent of the past but still inspiring to the present.

Jessica believes all pieces of furniture should have romantic character. A summer romance blossoms with her antique gilded iron console that brings the outside into your home. The leaf and vine decoration on the summer garden console were inspired from a garden gate at Jessica's home.

Somewhere In Time

Jessica's designs embody romantically shaped, soft, curved lines as shown in the dramatic sweep of the canopy bed and incorporate decorative motifs such as embroidery and jewelry. Her inspiration comes from traveling, studying art and collecting artifacts and books. In turn, we are encouraged to choose furnishings that reflect our own romantic interests and personality … lace accented linens, dramatic shapes and delicate carvings. We often hear her say that 'Romance' is beauty that touches the emotional part of our being.

Secret
trade

The exquisite hardware on the McClintock Collection is inspired by antique jewelry Jessica has collected. The pulls resemble broaches used to accessorize her apparel collections.

Inspired by antiques in Jessica's home, craftsmen have created timeless reproductions made from selected hardwoods, cherry veneers and marble. Flowering magnolias are the inspiration for the knobs on her writing desk which has lots of room to store papers, jewelry or collectibles. The writing surface is hand-tooled leather.

"Romantic character is accomplished by beautiful finishing, antique touches, bleached wood that looks old and worn, beautiful silk brocade or tapestry coverings."

Jessica McClintock

ox Rooms

Page 22-23: Jewel Box Rooms

Display your own jewel collections and fragrances in Jessica's Armoire. It is a faithful reproduction of one she has in her home in San Francisco. Its full-size mirror makes the room look more spacious. This is Jessica's favorite piece in the collection.

The Carriage Bed has many facets with its intricate shapes and soft, flowing curves. It's the jewel in any romantic bedroom.

Defining Desir

"Everything I design is influenced by my love of r o m a n t i c colors, tex-tures and lines."

Jessica McClintock

Jessica's garden table and chairs are a bouquet of flowers, vines and acanthus leaves which all add a Victorian touch.

The Trellis Deck and Demi-Lune (pictured left), with its leaf and vine motif in wrought iron, provide a romantic setting for a dinner buffet. Jessica's sunburst cherry veneer table, with its distinctive Victorian styling, sets the mood and the desire for formal entertaining.

etting Mood

The collection's style is defined by strong, dramatic pieces of furniture and beautiful wall finishes and moldings that romance the past. It pays great attention to detail. Personal antiques in Jessica's home inspired the Renaissance cocktail table and the credenza with oval mirror. Her French-style sofa, with a rayon damask that feels like silk, makes an elegant statement of the belle époque. Cherubs set the mood for Jessica's Romance Collection.

Return T

"Today's designers have made it possible for the consumer to define their varied lifestyles through the purchases they make. My collection offers the return to elegance in a very romantic way."

Jessica McClintock

Design
tip on

There is a similarity between the way people dress and the way they decorate. Make a statement with the articles in your home as you do with the garments you wear.

elegance

Emotional Touches *Of Beauty*

The Grand Hall console glitters with emotion that romances the past. It, too, is inspired by a piece in Jessica's home. It adds to the beauty of a magnificent work of art and welcomes guests to your home. Grandiose is the visual touch you derive from the heirloom silver leaf china cabinet. Reeded bun feet with egg and dart moldings add character to the room. The Garden Gate cocktail table accents this setting with a delicate and formal beauty.

Alexander Julian's fashion career began at age 16. He was the apparel manager for the family clothing store, Julian's College Shop, in Chapel Hill, North Carolina. He moved to New York City in 1975 to design menswear and was nominated for a Coty award the next year. In 1977, he won his first of five Coty awards. In 1981, he created "Colours by Alexander Julian", a menswear collection that has been an ongoing best seller. In 1994, in conjunction with Universal Furniture, Alex introduced his first furniture collection called Original. It was an immediate success and was followed by Chapel Hill in 1996, Patterns in 1998, Highlands and Sausalito in 2001. Each new collection has enhanced Alex's reputation for innovation, creativity, beauty and accessibility.

Alex is the quintessential Renaissance man. His designs have captivated the fashion, home furnishings, home décor, art and even the sports world. The brand umbrella, Alexander Julian At Home, includes wallcovering, paint, area rugs, decorative pillows, window treatments, wall-to-wall carpeting and laminate flooring. These products all reflect his philosophy that we should treat everyday as the weekend. His success is due in part to his ability to transform the ordinary into the extraordinary.

Alex's design talents lie in his ability to take traditional design motifs that are 'tried and true' and use them in a non-traditional application. He draws much of his inspiration from the fashion world of apparel. A good example is the argyle pattern … a timeless design. Wingtip curves and stitching, inspired by women's dress shoes from the 1920's and men's cowboy boots from the 1950's, make a classic 'arts & crafts' bed step out in extraordinary fashion.

Traditio

With A Twist

Fashion plays a big role in Alex's Original collection. With a blend of elegant cherry and casual pine woods, you can 'dress up' or 'dress down' a room.

The principle design elements are the cherry argyles and pine bowties on the elegantly shaped top of the dining room table. The graceful curves of the cabriole legs on the sleigh back chairs provide an elegant contrast to the sturdy rectangular legs of the table.

It Speaks Of Home

Great Scottish explorers traveled to China and returned with beautiful chinoiserie pieces. You can easily visualize yourself in a Scottish castle with the Balmoral Secretary (right) from Alex's Highlands collection. With its hand-painted chinoiserie decoration, this piece can be used as an accent with any style of furniture. The flowers and leaves are reminiscent of the changing shades of light on a castle wall in the hills of the Scottish highlands.

Casual an

Elegant All At Once

Pages 34-35: Casual And Elegant All At Once

Whether it's dinner after the backyard games or a feast for the clan during the holidays, every meal is a special occasion with the Tartan Trestle Table. A magnificent piece, it has sculptured, round pedestal columns and graceful cabriole legs with traditional acanthus leaf carvings.

The Highlands Refectory Sideboard recalls an authentic piece from a Scottish estate. It is the perfect companion for any gathering. Elegantly set for tea or laden with spoils of the hunt, the Scottish oak burl veneers and sweater cable accents are always in proper attire.

trade Secret

Alex's Scottish ancestors settled in the Carolinas in the late 1700's. Many of his award-winning sweaters and tweeds were made from the rich cashmeres and wools of Scotland. You'll spot plaids, argyles and cable patterns in his furniture pieces. Even the brass hardware carries the Scottish thistle design.

If you like the idea of combining traditional Scottish elements with a 'fashion' approach, the Highlander Poster Bed has three large diamond argyle motifs on the headboard, fancy faced burl veneers and reeding supported by 'sweater cable' tall posts.

Filled With Romance And Drama

People Smile And Enjoy Life

Alex's most recent collection, Sausalito, was inspired by his wife Megan's hometown. He found this northern California community to be a rich and expressive fusion of Eastern and Western cultures, sophistication and romance, architecture and nature, eucalyptus and bamboo. Sausalito combines all these elements. The eclectic harmony of this collection invites relaxation in any environment … rural or urban. It will always find a home where people smile and enjoy life.

Alex shows us how to 'dress up' furniture with custom-designed hardware on his Storefront Hutch. He uses antiqued sterling silverplate which mimics actual jewelry.

Bamboo, one of nature's most durable sculptures, has captivated designers since its "discovery." Some of the pieces from the Sausalito collection combine fancy face bamboo veneers and woven wicker for a Far East fashion statement.

With their soft curves, the Trident Table and Jocelyn Chairs (right) are both elegant and casual.

Alex's goal is to make it easy for you to express yourself in a comfortable manner. He designs furniture he hopes will be used and enjoyed for many years. Take inspiration from your travels, celebrate your heritage and take pleasure in your family and life experiences. Alex believes we should try and live as if every day is the weekend.

"I choose to work with the two main areas of personal self-expression: fashion and home furnishings. How we dress and how we 'feather our nests' contribute so much to each of our personal well being."

Alexander Julian

Every Day Is The Weekend

Kathy draws upon her experience as a wife and mother of two to help today's families turn their living spaces into homes. Chief Designer and CEO of Kathy Ireland WorldWide, she began her business and design career in 1993, literally from the ground up, with a collection of socks. Today, Kathy brings to her customer affordable, stylish and practical fashions that are comparable to those found on the world's most recognized runways. She is dedicated to maintaining an open dialog with her primarily female audience whom she serves by providing a constant feedback to their questions submitted via her website. In 2002, Standard Furniture became lead partner for Kathy Ireland Home, which was an immediate success.

Kathy Ireland first gained recognition as a supermodel, appearing on the cover of countless magazines, including Glamour, Cosmopolitan, Harper's Bazaar and Sports Illustrated. Utilizing experience gained from her travels all over the world, and inspired by working with many talented designers, Kathy developed her Home Collection with the mission of finding solutions for families, especially busy moms. Her Home Collection includes furniture, rugs, carpet, tile, lamps, art, kitchenware and other home products. It offers comfortable, casual and elegant offerings that coordinate with a wide range of home decors.

Coming Home T

Coming home to Kathy's Island Paradise Collection is like escaping on a mini vacation. The deep cherry finish and vertical reeding on each of the pieces are visible reminders of their island inspiration. The versatility of this collection allows it to be at home in a masculine décor, or it can be accessorized for the most feminine of boudoirs.

omfort

Inspired by the luxury and grandeur of Italian palazios, the Via D'Amore grouping makes an impressive presentation with its carvings of acanthus leaves, rope twists and delicate florettes, as well as gold tipping and serpentine shapes.

Kathy has combined wood, marble and resin castings to create the look of Italian designs in the Via D'Amore dining and occasional furniture. The Kathy Ireland Home Collection also offers a selection of rug patterns that speak any language. They are the passport to your own design destination.

Bellisimo .

For a regal look, the Palace bedroom is a virtual symphony of movement with the serpentine chest and dresser fronts and metal scrollwork on the headboard and footboard. Providing a secret hiding place, the dresser features a hidden drawer for concealing precious jewelry and valuables. You'll definitely feel like royalty when you retire to the Via D'Amore master suite. The detailed, ornate design elements in this group are a tribute to Italian artistry.

or Every Room

Priva

Quarters

Your Year Fo

Comfort and elegance reign with Kathy's Palace Master Suite. This formal interpretation of the sleigh bed gives you a grand look that has been scaled for today's home.

The Family Get-Together

The gentle hills and fields of England provide the classic, elegant influence for Kathy's British Countryside Collection … matched veneers, floral motifs and pilasters that resemble classical columns. This is furniture that is timeless … and timely.

The type of entertaining you do is an important consideration when selecting furniture for your dining room. Some of us entertain once a month … others for family reunions only once a year. The Kathy Ireland Home Collection offers both style and function whether for the family's evening gathering or when it's your turn to host a holiday celebration.

trade Secret

Just as we add accessories for visual interest and to establish a definite theme for a room, a designer does the same thing to a piece of furniture by using carvings, appliqués and wood grains to create visual drama.

As a wife and mother, Kathy understands a family's need for each member to feel special in their own personal space. Whether your princess is holding court or dreaming a fairytale, the Princess Bouquet Youth Group has all the right subjects.

A common thread woven throughout Kathy's furniture is its practical and well-mannered appearance. Her youth bedroom has easy-to-clean surfaces that can withstand ice cream drips, spills, and crayons and still look terrific when the 'little princess' has sleepover guests.

The pieces in this group are adorned with flower bouquet designs that resemble hand-painted artistry. They have been designed with both function and safety in mind. There is a wall mount on the back of the chest to prevent tip over. The student desk has removable and adjustable shelving that offers added storage flexibility.

Kathy understands the importance of capturing special moments in a family's evolution. Her youth group moves from toddler to teen without the growing pains.

For Kathy, "Comfort is no longer a trend … it's a revolution that families demand." Whether it's clothes or home furnishings, Kathy's designs follow the belief that we want comfort in every aspect of our busy lives. Kathy believes that the most valuable time we have is the time spent at home with our families. Kathy's sofas and chairs are great for cuddling, whether with your spouse, your child or a good book.

In her travels, Kathy has experienced firsthand many cultures, landscapes, homes and historical places. Inspiration for her collection comes from various world destinations such as England, Italy, France, Spain and the Middle East. With old world wood pieces and richly textured upholstered seating, it is apparent that fine antiques inspire many of her designs.

Hand-painted designs, typically crafted by native artisans, are now accessible to everyone in the Colección Mis Flores Amor and Grand Legacy groupings.

The hand-painted designs of the Colección Mis Flores group are just as comfortable in the bedroom as they are classy in the living room. Whether your decorating scheme calls for a linen armoire or an entertainment center, the common thread in Kathy Ireland's Collection is versatility and practicality.

Design
tip on

Remember to create conversation areas in the room. A good rule of thumb is to try to maintain no more than eight feet of distance between furniture pieces in your conversation area to allow people to comfortably carry on a conversation while seated.

As a young boy growing up in Southern California, Mackie submerged himself in Hollywood glamour by seeing and studying every film he could lay his eyes on. After leaving design school, he was ready to attack Hollywood and was soon in great demand as an assistant to many of the industry's top designers, including the famed Edith Head.

By the mid-60's Mackie was the hot young 'mod' designer and was designing costumes for many of the top television variety specials featuring such stars as Fred Astaire, Mitzi Gaynor, Dinah Shore and Dianna Ross and The Supremes. In 1967, after seeing Mitzi Gaynor in her Mackie-designed Las Vegas show, Joe Hamilton immediately hired Mackie to design all of the costumes for the Carol Burnett Show. His career has since spanned a myriad of fashion products. He even added a touch of the Mackie glamour to the young set with his highly coveted collectible Barbie Doll series. Bob's furniture is destined to be a star because he uses his fashion know-how to create show-stopping silhouettes and character pieces that support the glamour in any room.

Man of many talents, Bob Mackie is perhaps best known for the costumes he designed for the 11-year run of the Carol Burnett Show. After guest starring on the Burnett Show, Cher also became one of Bob's biggest fans. The outrageously glamorous clothes Mackie created for her soon became one of the biggest draws on weekly television. Bob garnered seven Emmy Awards as well as the 1999 Costume Designers Guild Award. In 1982 he created a ready-to-wear line that rapidly grew into other fashion-related products throughout the 80's and 90's. In 1998, Mackie entered the world of home furnishings when he launched a furniture collection for American Drew, a La-Z-Boy company.

Bob Mackie

Bob's philosophy of design is that whatever he creates must always be appropriate for its time, place and function. Whether designing a dress or a piece of furniture, it has to be beautiful and functional.

Just like the opening scene in a show, the foyer or entry is the plot setter for your home. The Plume Chest with marble top and silver leaf finish will impress, entertain and induce a little envy. If you're looking for drama, the bombe chest will be noticed wherever it is playing.

Dares To B

Noticed

The upholstered pieces in the Bob Mackie Collection take their cue from the Hollywood glamour of the 20's and 30's. The opulent, overstuffed, loose pillow look evokes the sensuality of the period. Bob revives this legacy with fashions for the home.

The Runway cocktail table combines wood, glass and metal to create visual interest.

The round lamp table is made of the same mix of contrasting materials. The design trade refers to this as 'mixed media.' Both the cocktail table and the lamp table have a lower shelf to display additional items.

Hollywood Breeding

"My furniture collection reflects a romantic and gracious time past with the practical luxury and comfort of today. These pieces will become the coveted heirlooms of tomorrow."

Bob Mackie

Elegance And Romance

Bob Mackie's designs echo his perception of comfort and luxury. A home truly becomes yours when you combine beautiful colors, beautiful woods, beautiful fabrics with your personal treasures. Gracious living is the objective. Bob suggests you select a piece, like this cocktail table with its generously carved legs and beveled glass top, to be the focal point for intimate entertaining.

Secret trade

"The basic design principles that I use in clothing worked exactly the same with this collection. Even the hardware is like the buckles and buttons on a garment. Whether clothes or furniture, everything needs the perfect accent and finishing touch. In fact, throughout my fashion career, my designs have often been influenced by architecture and period ornamentation, so I guess I am coming full circle."

Bob Mackie

To complete this setting, the 'Isabella' sofa, in chenille, is properly accessorized with tapestry pillows, heavily fringed in silk. Just as a woman might select a pin or a broach to accent her attire, Bob throws in an odd pillow to add the illusion of something you might have run across in an antique shop.

Chenille has become a luxuriously appealing fabric for today's upholstery. Weaving and finishing techniques elevate this fabric from a supporting to a starring role. Mixing fabric textures will entertain the eye and draw spontaneous applause from your guests.

Glamourou

Legendary Flair For Style

Page 60-61: Glamourous ... Charismatic

Marrying fashion to furnishings, the Opera Table and Plume Mirror are embellished with custom woven bracelet hardware, embroidered button rosettes and imported marble from Spain. They are the quintessential pieces in any setting.

Bob's fashion acumen struts its charm and glamour into the bedroom. His panel bed has sleek lines and graceful curves. The pierced cartouche 'S' scroll crown adorns the headboard. His bedroom group delivers its lines with a French accent and an anticipation of romance.

Sleigh beds have been in vogue for decades but they have never been more popular than the present. The Sleigh Bed is Bob's signature piece. He delights in designing curves and shapes into his furniture. The rooms you keep to yourself are quite often most reflective of your personal style. Fashion truly begins and ends in the bedroom. Remember, your bedroom is the last thing you see at the end of a glorious evening and the first thing you see when you awake.

"I believe that your home is your haven – your sanctuary – a place to get away from the rest of the world. A home should be comfortable, with a sense of your own history, with treasured things you have gathered over the years that define who you are and help personalize your environment."

Bob Mackie

Your home can have a sense of fantasy. It can be a Moraccan palace, a Spanish colonial villa or a French Château – whatever pleases you. Home is where you can control your surroundings and be transported into your own private world as soon as you enter the front door.

The versatile buffet, or server, is a mainstay in any well dressed home. It can embellish the foyer, the dining room or most any area of the home. For a show-stopping venue, 'overdone' can work well with the right, elegant pieces. Bob's Bunching Curio Cabinets deliver an outrageous finale to a sensational gathering.

Opulent Embellishmen

"I always advise a client to know themselves and what they really want, whether it be on their bodies or in their homes. Be an individual; don't follow the herd. Decide what pleases you and what's best on and around you."

Bob Mackie

Outrageously Beautiful

In 2000, Kincaid Furniture, a La-Z-Boy company, introduced the Laura Ashley Home Collection. Laura Ashley was a romantic who found inspiration in nature and the past. She created an idyllic vision of the countryside, distilling the essence of English Romanticism and giving it a vitality that has delighted millions.

The Laura Ashley style evokes a timeless mood of peace and serenity. Its focal point is the home and the family. The atmosphere it creates is one of warmth and welcome whether the home is a rosy Cotswold cottage or a terraced house in the city. It recalls the days when everything was crafted from local natural materials, sturdy enough to last for life and be passed down to the next generation.

Laura Ashley's home furnishings are inspired by both Victorian and 19th Century French Designs. The dramatic Westchester Bed is illustrative of Laura's formal flair. Sleep in the inherited style of the English upper class. Hand carvings accent all of the pieces in the collection. They add a refined character to the bedroom.

Laura Ashley was born in Wales in 1925. When Audrey Hepburn sported a headscarf in the 1953 film Roman Holiday, it created a style that became an instant hit around the globe. It was exactly at that time that a young couple, Laura and Bernard Ashley , began producing headscarves, as well as tablemats and napkins, on their kitchen table in a flat in Pimlico. The Ashley scarves were an instant success with stores such as John Lewis and Heal's. The Ashleys were now on their way to becoming a company which has annual sales of over $500 million with more than 530 shops worldwide. However, tragedy was to strike without warning. In 1985, on her 60th birthday, Laura fell down the stairs and was rushed to the hospital where she died ten days later.

Laura Ashley

To Th

Manor Born

Laura's Keswick poster bed and bedside chest echo the flowing styles of her clothing designs. Deep fluting, hand carved leaves, carved tulip feet, flower and vine carvings mirror Laura's collection of designs and fabric patterns from museums she has visited around the world.

Posing as the proper English woman, in a high-necked blouse of luxurious fabric, the Westchester group sets a style that recalls the Victorian ritual of an afternoon retreat. Pamper yourself while seated at Laura's vanity. The vanity, with its tilt mirror, reprises an elegant statement in today's bedroom. It's best to position this piece so natural light can illuminate your face for daytime makeup. Evening cosmetic applications take on a romantic allure with a table light that is soft and is no taller than when you are seated.

An Englishwoman

The Camberly cocktail table is the perfect spot for afternoon tea - whether in a bedroom sitting area or the living room.

etreat

Classic Grace, Wit And Charm

The dining room furniture in Laura's collection adds both a charming and a graceful style to your entertaining. Mix the off-white antique linen finished pieces with the antique brown Heirloom ones for a lighthearted decor. The Snowdon pedestal table is comfortable in a traditional country setting with its crackled finish. Borrow a decorating trait from our English relatives and add a casual basket of flowers from the garden. This is the "correct" setting for young ladies to acquire the proper hostess skills.

trade Secret

Careful attention is given to hand carved details such as bell flowers, rosettes, and acanthus leaf overlays. In 19th Century France and England, heavy ornamentation was the mark of success and upper class.

Dappled Rituals

Formality gives way to unpretentious style even in the all Heirloom finished dining room. The traditional Sunday Brunch is quintessential Laura Ashley.

Laura's insistence on a simplistic lifestyle allows all the pieces in her collection to be mixed and matched. Classic English Country blends with a touch of Louis Philippe in the morning sun.

The 18th and 19th centuries produced art and literature which are now called 'Romantic.' The landscapes and scenes of country life by Turner and Constable were revolutionary in showing ordinary people and everyday tasks. The poetry of that era is captured in the fabrics of the Laura Ashley Home Collection.

Visualize yourself in the tranquility of Laura's country cottage, overlooking the green, Welsh farmland. The floral patterns of her printed textiles transport you to fields of inspiration.

Beyond The Summer

A room comes alive when Laura's style is applied to home furnishings décor. Her colors and prints delight the eye and dress the room in English charm. Adding the fragrance of flowers and potpourri further enhances this visual impression.

The Laura Ashley Home Collection captures the essence of a shared history. From formal to cottage chic, you can make pageantry and glamour a part of your everyday life. The furniture pieces in the collection compliment each other and characterize a room like the preface in a great novel. A single piece can add a touch of English wit or take you nostalgically back to the past. This collection has the proper attire for any occasion.

On fabric prints, a window sill or a formal dinner setting, an English Garden bouquet is the trademark of Laura Ashley.

tip on
Design

The Laura Ashley style comes from a mix of different patterns. The key to achieving this look is to use one or two common colors throughout the space. To avoid a 'busy' look, vary the scale of the patterns.

Whiffles C

Thomas Kinkade is an accomplished modern-day romantic realist and America's most-collected living artist. He communicates through paintings whose tranquil, light-infused subjects project a theme of hope and joy. This has earned him the sobriquet 'the painter of light'. Kinkade believes that each painting he creates is a quiet messenger in the home whose purpose is to affirm the basic values of family, faith in God and the luminous beauty of nature. His goal as an artist is to touch people of all faiths, to bring peace and joy into their lives through the images he creates.

It was while growing up in the small town of Placerville, California that these simple, life-affirming values were instilled in him. As a young man he began to explore the world around him, experimenting with the effects of light and shadow. It was during this time that Thomas took a sketching tour with a college friend, producing the best-selling instructional book, *The Artist's Guide to Sketching*. Six years in a row Kinkade was named Graphic Artist of the Year by the National Association of Limited Edition Dealers, as well as the Collectors Editions Award of Excellence. He was a charter inductee, along with his idol, Norman Rockwell, to the Bradford International Hall of Fame for plate artists. He was inducted into the U.S. Art Hall of Fame in 1999. His images can be found on a wide array of home accessories, gifts and collectibles. In 1998, two divisions of La-Z-Boy, Inc., La-Z-Boy Residential and Kincaid Furniture Company (no relation) entered into a licensing partnership to produce exclusive lines of home furnishings inspired by Kinkade's popular images.

Invite your guests to alfresco dining with this garden-inspired group made with warm wood and antique pewter finished metal. The baker's rack is the perfect compliment for serving a continental breakfast or displaying your collectibles.

It is light that first draws you to Thomas Kinkade's paintings. This same luminosity has been translated in the warm finishes of his furniture collection. His "romantic realism" is translated in the exclusive fabrics available on the collection's upholstery pieces.

Kinkade delights in simple images that are pleasing to the eye. We see this in the soft, scalloped lines and cabriole legs of his occasional tables. The Whitney sofa, with generous proportion and sloping arms, adds an old English style to the setting. It helps deliver a sophisticated and comfortable greeting to all who enter the room.

The graceful arching bridge of 'Lamplight Inn' invites us to partake of the hospitality that promises to refresh our spirits inside this spacious old country inn.

trade Secret

A devoted husband and doting father, Kinkade hides the letter 'N' in each of his paintings to pay tribute to his wife Nanette. In keeping with his artwork theme, the letter 'N' is also hidden in select pieces of furniture.

A Bright Homecoming

The same graceful lines appear on the harvest table and welcome the family to this season's feast. Its versatile design lights up with a formal affair or the daily meals.

Page 82-83: All Aglow With Morning

Rise and shine in European style with the Spring Gate Bed. Headboard finials resemble lanterns and Kinkade's painting, *Spring Gate*, inspires the metalwork. You can easily create a chateau environment for the master suite or guest bedroom.

With Morning

"Furniture is a lot like art. People bring it into their houses to make their surroundings more beautiful and to create that special sanctuary we call 'home.' Both can enhance and affirm a family's time together."

Thomas Kinkade

Sun Dancin

'Lamplight Bridge' is enlivened by the vibrant glitter of gas lamps. The ancient stone span links neighbors...and enhances the cozy hospitality of English country living.

Kinkade's furniture reflects the same traditions of family and the comfort of home he creates in his paintings. He draws a parallel between the work he does as a painter and the talent of the artisan who crafts each bed and dresser out of solid wood.

The Merritt Drawer Chest (left) is named for one of Thomas Kinkade's daughters. Its unique design feature is the overhanging top drawer. It's the perfect 'anywhere' piece that accommodates sweaters, lingerie or guest linens. Thomas readily admits to having been inspired by his wife and children when designing this piece.

A sleigh bed is always a style focus in the room. The open slats on the head and foot boards of Kinkade's sleigh bed filter the sun's light with a musical accent.

Shadows

Kinkade lives the life his paintings depict ... a simpler life, rooted in family, faith and the serenity of nature. This is a theme he repeats regularly in his furniture designs.

The Gatsby sofa and Spindale high-leg lounger take your decorating scheme back to a time when in-home entertaining was the fashion and styles were classic, with details that have gracefully aged into modern interpretations.

Reflections C

Spring Gate' portrays a massive wrought iron gate framed by stone pillars. Spring and nature are rejuvenated with a magnificent display of floral perfection.

Once again, Kinkade's talent for combining aesthetically-pleasing looks with functional practicality is validated by the square cocktail table. It has a hidden storage area and two working drawers. The lid is hinged so that it is easy to store or remove items. The cabriole legs are Kinkade's signature design element.

tip on
Design

For a nostalgic theme, add old leather-bound books to your display cabinet ... use vintage model boats or sailing ships as accents.

esterday

A devout Christian and family man, Thomas Kinkade draws on personal experience for much of his artistic inspiration. A style rich with memories and family-friendly attitudes, each piece in the Thomas Kinkade Collection is an escape to life's simple pleasures. The Chalet sofa and Washington high-leg recliner create a welcome retreat from the outside world. Add a little country cottage charm with the wood and scrolled metal cocktail table.

A Direct Source Of Style

The Lamplight China Base is at home in the den, foyer or living room. It sets the style tempo for any area. The themes of peace and tranquility are always present in Kinkade's furnishings. It's style that is as generous and classy as its creator.

"Thank you for considering inviting us into your home … it is truly an honor. May you enjoy these furnishings as much as we have enjoyed bringing them to you and may you and your family enjoy God's bountiful blessings in your home."

Thomas Kinkade

The Joe Ruggiero Collection is a streamlined group of furniture, fabrics and decorative accessories that provides a framework for designing every room in the home. It's an easy, sophisticated look based on the philosophy that people should have a comfortable foundation of home furnishings they can build on, grow with, move from room to room and add to over time.

Ruggiero is well known for his ability to identify what homeowners are looking for and show them how to create it from both an aesthetic and practical point of view. He has proven to be an expert authority in identifying international trends and translating them into design ideas. His multi-media work has reached millions who welcome him into their homes weekly. He has become a familiar face that people trust to guide them through the decorating stages of their lives.

Joe Ruggiero's expertise in creating stylish and sophisticated environments that are affordable for people from all walks of life is the result of having worked directly with consumers for almost 30 years. He has been Advertising Director for West Point Pepperell and Ethan Allen; a national spokesperson for Glidden, Ethan Allen and Kohler; host and producer of the "Kohler Radio Series"; Editor-In-Chief and Publishing Director of Home Magazine; host and producer of HGTV's Homes Across America, viewed weekly by 60 million households. For nine years he was Chief Design Consultant to the PBS award-winning series, This Old House. He also spent two years as Design Correspondent on ABC-TV's Good Morning America.

Joe is the author of the design and source book, Found Objects and in 1995 was the recipient of the International Furnishings and Design Association (IFDA) Star of the Year award. In the spring of 2000, he launched the Joe Ruggiero Collection for Norwalk Furniture.

Uptown Fashio

Who says New York City has to be in New York? With Boulevard, you can enjoy an uptown look in your own home. The style is sleek, sophisticated and modern. An English fireplace fender was the inspiration for the Talmadge Cocktail Table. Just changing the tabletop from wood to tufted leather can set the mood of the room and take you from Milan to London. Joe creates a global fashion look by mixing materials such as chrome and mahogany, fabric and leather.

New York, Milan, Paris

Joe has chosen 'celebrity' names for his furniture. The Swanson table (left) was inspired by a farm implement he found in a Japanese village. The table is versatile enough to star in the dining room, the library, the foyer or in the bedroom. The Pickford dining chair was inspired by a Swedish antique Joe found in Barcelona. With its timeless design, it lends elegance to any dinner setting.

Genre Of Slee

The Crawford Demi Lune Table is a salute to Hollywood during the 1930's. Its dramatic curved lines play to the architecture of that era, as well as to the design of Joe's collection. The Crawford table makes a lovely bedside table, hall piece, sofa table or accent piece for any room.

Modular seating allows for great flexibility. The Hopper chair can adapt to any room … contemporary or traditional. It can pose a sleek, solid look or be grouped with single armless chairs to create a more modern arrangement. The Brooks triple dresser in the background serves multiple functions in the bedroom, the dining room or in the hall.

ity Shapes

Inspired by Louis XVI, who revolutionized cleaner lines in French design, the Chevalier chair sets a Euro-Country style for the dining room, the boudoir or anywhere in the home.

tip on Design

"I had been thinking of demystifying and simplifying the process of decorating for consumers for years. The concept of a basic wardrobe that can be transformed with pattern, texture and color as it travels through different design themes makes so much sense today ... and has been undiscovered by our industry."

Joe Ruggiero

As basic as the little black dress, the Bergen, Joe's interpretation of the classic Bergère, an 18th Century upholstered French armchair, takes on a country aire with the right fabric or wood finish. Joe looks to Provence for fabric inspirations, including a rich matelasse for a French Provencal quilt based on an antique tapestry and lavish garden print linen bed drapings with sunkissed dahlias.

Joe adds a contemporary twist by taking the traditional Lawson sofa, adding a dramatic arched arm, tight back and "Ruggiero-style" legs. The couture style French fold arm and center welt add fresh design direction to a sophisticated country theme.

Overlookin

Page 96-97: Overlooking London's High Street

Each piece in the Powell Group features loose seat cushions, semi-attached back and lumbar pillows on an architectural frame. Note the elegantly curved arm and stylishly carved walnut feet that would be at home in a London studio.

How about embellishing your home with the exotic … a hint of Morocco, India, Thailand and the Orient. Ruggiero's Spice Collection evokes a sense of mystery and a passion for rich color. The theme conveys intense color rather than pattern. He uses large print fabric, designs we don't often have the courage to try … shades of island color, Chinese red and fuchsia, cumin and curry. You will find upholstered pieces in silk-like faille with subtle stripes, as well as luxe-checked cottons.

Joe's love of the deep reds of Hong Kong and Morocco, the natural linens with large Tahitian tropical plants, the ethnic cottons and silks woven with subtle layers of island colors are the flavors of his Spice Collection. Some of the patterns are traditional block print patterns based on Moroccan tiles and friezes.

The Spice Route

Others are India-inspired sari patterns, expensive Thai silks in rich plaids, and sumptuous Spice Island chenille and cottons that evoke a mysterious mélange that pervades the collection's exotic spirit.

Fabrics in the Garden Collection, as well as the Euro-Country Collection, are anything but refined and muted. Ruggiero's visit to the Jackie Kennedy fashion retrospective in New York inspired his own translations to intense color and garden themes. Giant blooms and landscaping images are everywhere. They extend to toile designs featuring engraved urns and leaves, fanciful poppy printed cottons, gingham and trelliswork settings. This collection also features four-panel photographs of antique roses in full bloom from Ruggiero's personal garden.

On the following page you catch the corner of the Fitzgerald desk, a campaign desk much like the one used by Napoleon in his travels. The desk was designed from a piece Joe has in his own collection. It is equally at home as a bedside table, dressing table, sofa table or accent piece in the entry hall.

"In such times as we're in right now, we'll seek the peace and serenity of the garden. It's where nature brings new life, color and tranquility, a natural refuge."

Joe Ruggiero

Peace & Serenit

tip on
Design

As was the tradition in the French court, the more expensive fabric was placed on the front of the chair and a less expensive fabric was tailored on the back. Use this pattern play theory to establish the style impact of any room.

f the Garden

Chris Madden has designed rooms for a variety of clients, including Katie Couric, Toni Morrison and Oprah Winfrey. She spends a great deal of her time traveling the world, exploring the side streets of New York, Paris, Venice and Istanbul, as well as off-the-beaten-path design sources, like flea markets, to have a consumer's vision of which objects and colors work well together in the home. Chris uses a variety of finishes and textures to create unique looks. She likes to mix contrasting materials like metal and wood, rattan and leather, to make you feel as if you have discovered an antique shop overflowing with interesting finds. Her philosophy is to have fun … discover a style all your own. Chris conveys this knowledge in a very understandable manner in her weekly prime time show on HGTV's Interiors By Design. She also writes a syndicated column for more than 300 newspapers. In April 2000, Chris debuted her collection for Bassett, one of the nation's largest furniture companies.

Chris Madden lives in Westchester County, New York with her husband, Kevin, their two sons, Patrick and Nick and their two West Highland Terriers, Winnie and Lola. She and Kevin have more than 30 years combined design experience. Chris has written and published 15 books, eight on home design. In addition to her media appearances, speeches and articles, she has contributed her time to numerous charities including Habitat for Humanity, Quilts For Kids and The Kips Bay Boys and Girls Club Decorator Show House.

Chris prefers a relaxed and eclectic look to create a mood that is very personal and intimate. The four-poster metal Cassone Bed and Butche Table, with their burnished bronze patina and bamboo regency styling, demonstrate the versatility of the Chris Madden Collection. Taking its style from the British Colonial era, it can create a unique look for any home … whether a sleek city loft, a rambling traditional Georgian two-story or a Cape Cod Saltbox.

A Personal Style A

our Own

Chris shows how to create an ambience that exudes warmth and charm by using natural textures like wicker and rattan. The glass top rattan dining table and arm chairs in a setting of whitewashed walls, exposed beams and wainscoting, create the coastal feeling … a look that is rapidly gaining in popularity. Simplicity is the key element.

ache

Every room can use the natural look of a plant or two. The addition of greenery, as well as brightly colored flowering plants, can really bring a room to life and add texture and pattern to the décor.

The Anacapri Cupboard (right) is a casual and comfortable addition to the dining room or family room. It's an accent piece that can turn a home into a sunlit waterfront cottage.

Chris designed her collection to make it easy for you to create a unique look for your own home. With its variety of finishes and textures, you'll feel like you've discovered an antique shop overflowing with wonderful finds. Mix metal and wood, rattan and leather. And most of all – have fun!! Discover a style all your own.

The Cottage Style is all about living with ease … about space and light. Sunlight streams into this living room and envelops it. It becomes a cozy place to entertain or simply relax.

Most of us seek a warm and cozy place in the home to steal away to. This South Seas Cottage Collection is elegantly casual but most of all comfortable. Selecting and placing decorative items is a great way to express your personality. Family photos, personal mementos from trips, favorite collections, all serve as meaningful accents while simultaneously adding interest and warmth to the room. When you surround yourself with objects that evoke pleasant memories, you are also revealing your personal style to others.

A Good Book And Earl Grey Tea

hat's Traditional

Pages 108-109: All That's Traditional

If you like an open floor plan, the Grand Home Collection incorporates all the pieces needed for this style of living … for family room, dining room, home office and even the media room. Intricate detailing, gentle distressing and graceful silhouettes give each piece the appearance of a timeworn treasure.

Whether special occasions call for a dinner party or simply an intimate gathering for two, the dining collection provides a beautiful setting in which to celebrate. The Beau Brummel server is especially useful for large get-togethers or buffets. Its inspiration comes from the original beau brummel in Chris' home and dates back to the turn-of-the-century.

Special Occasio

If you are selecting furniture that can be used for more than one purpose, this pedestal table and upholstered chairs can be used for either formal dining or a casual dinner for two. It might also be a game table. This comes from Chris' philosophy that your home should represent you. Pick up an interesting vase at an estate sale. Warm up your hardwood floors with an oriental rug that was an anniversary gift from your spouse. Spice up your bookshelves with an antique tin box inherited from your great aunt. Frame and hang a gallery of old family photos in a grouping down a hallway. Your home will then become a reflection of your personality and your tastes. A home should be a place you like to come back to … to be with friends, family or just by yourself.

Secret trade

Shopping for accessories should be fun. Rooms that are accessorized at the same time look that way. Uniform. Almost too planned out. A truly interesting home is one that has been decorated over time.

"Whatever your style, all the pieces I've designed will blend nicely with your décor."

Chris Madden

More than any other room, the bedroom reflects your deepest passions and thoughts. We tend to select colors, shapes, even aromas, brought from our childhood. The romantic Mayflower Poster Bed looks like it may have been lovingly passed down through several generations. The rustic style kindles a longing to invoke the past, connect with nature, relax, and rekindle our dreams.

Chris loves to bring warmth and character to all corners of the home. The Maréchal LeClerc Armoire is not only a beautiful piece of furniture, its drawers are cedar lined to protect clothing, or it can be used as a home entertainment center.

"A home should be a reflection of your personality, your tastes and your soul," says Chris. "How your home looks should nurture and welcome you. It's my favorite place to be."

"The rustic beauty of this collection soothes the spirit with a tonic of space, light, warmth and repose."

Chris Madden

In 1883 Claude Monet moved with his family to Giverny, a small village not far from Paris. He lived there until he died in 1926 at the age of 86. Monet designed the entire setting at Giverny. The house, the studio, the gardens and the ponds all served as continual inspiration for his work. Most of his best-known paintings, the famous Water Lilies and the popular Haystack series, were created at Giverny.

Impressionist

Monet

If you visit Giverny, you will see Monet's influence in every room of his home … from the unique paint colors (which he viewed as architectural elements), to the china patterns he designed for his personal dining.

Perhaps Monet's real masterpieces were his gardens, which he arranged like a palette by organizing the flower banks in bright magical tones to dazzle the eye. Monet used nature as his studio and drew upon his gardens to create the impressionistic strokes of luminosity and color that define his paintings.

Today, the house and gardens have been painstakingly restored to recreate the setting that Monet viewed daily. Each year, for the seven months it is open, Giverny receives more than one million visitors and is the most frequented site in Normandy.

In the pages to follow, you will see furniture from Habersham's Claude Monet Collection. Habersham is a leading manufacturer of hand-painted and hand-finished furniture. Their master artists have sought to capture the spirit of the great Impressionist and his celebrated home in their collection of individually hand-painted designs.

Create some drama with this stunning armoire depicting Monet's 1873 painting, *Artist's House at Argenteuil*. The doors open to reveal a pattern reminiscent of the blue and white tile found in Monet's home in Giverny. The armoire is available in a choice of interior options … with adjustable shelves, with drawers for use as a clothes closet or in a home office configuration.

Inspired by Monet's painting, *Gladioli*, this sideboard can serve dual function as a media cabinet or a serving center. The doors open to reveal an eloquent, hand-painted quote from the French poet, Octave Mirbeau, celebrating the beauty of the gladioli.

"*Here and there, rising from this marvelous wave, this marvelous flow of flowers, the gladioli dress these masts with exquisitely rumpled fabrics, as light and vaporous as gauze, their creases satin-brilliant; they bear little dancer skirts that balloon and billow.*"

Octave Mirbeau, 19th century French poet,
on Claude Monet's garden, 1891

The stately and eloquent Louis XV Bibliotheque is an example of the decidedly French style in which Monet chose to furnish his home. Monet's 1874 painting, *Le Déjeuner (The Luncheon)*, inspired the chest. Habersham's artists have selected colors from Monet's bedroom to create the delicate, hand-painted elements along the legs, front and sides of the chest.

The Kitche

lues

tip on Design

Light and color set the mood of a room. They can be soothing or energetic. Monet once told the French painter, Courbet, that he would not paint even the leaves in the background unless the lighting conditions were just right. When creating the mood in your own room vignette, use the Master's technique to see how both natural and artificial light affect its luminosity and ambience.

RRRRRibbitt

Page 118-119: The Kitchen Blues

The intricate designs on the meticulously painted tabletop mimic the blue tiles found in Monet's kitchen. The blue tones also echo those of the famed Blue Salon at Giverny. The style and colors of the chairs replicate those found in Monet's dining room.

Celebrating Monet's love of the French countryside, this piece reflects furnishings found in homes throughout and surrounding the Provence region of France. The trumeau mirrors above the sideboard were inspired by Monet's *Water Lilies* series. You can almost hear frogs croaking in the pond as your eye is drawn to the soft, delicate brush strokes and the rich color palette of the hand-painted piece.

Like Monet, Habersham's artists look to the bright magical tones given off by the irises of Giverny's flower banks to create the impressionistic strokes of luminosity and color that decorate this grand scale design. The green hues and soft tones are reminiscent of Monet's epicerie room at Giverny.

"More than anything I must have flowers always, always."

Claude Monet

The blue and white tiles and tones that flow throughout Monet's Giverny home are reflected in the delicate patterns and hues which adorn this stunning hutch design. It is called the Blue and White Toile cupboard. Rustic screens in the doors provide added texture. The cupboard offers a generous amount of shelf storage space.

Flowers were Monet's favorite still-life subject. It's the closest he came to figurative art in the sense of a centered form standing out against its background.

The Garde

You can sleep in the style of the Old Master himself. Reflecting the design of Monet's own bed, it can transform any bedroom into a garden room at Giverny.

Walk beside the stone path, enter the green-framed doors and bring the garden into your home. Each of the doors on the sideboard features a hand-painted flower drawing upon a rich palette of reds, yellows, pinks and purples. There are hand-painted design accents that highlight the sides, base and top of the piece as well.

You inherit the Country Estate lifestyle with this spectacular canopy bed. Picture yourself in a romantic French country setting with Claude Monet painting one of his masterpieces in the garden.

"I've been to Giverny and during the visit I found myself even more inspired by this remarkable artist. We are honored to have been chosen to participate in this exciting collection and we look forward to creating new designs that pay tribute to his work and reflect the great joy Monet obviously took in creating his warm, inspiring home environment."

Joyce Eddy, Founder/Chairman, Habersham

"You have reached the absolute beauty of great decoration."

Octave Mirbeau, 19th century French poet

Along the Stone Wall

Resource Guide

Pages 90-101

JOE RUGGIERO
COLLECTION

Furniture
Norwalk Furniture
Corporation
877-770-3483
www.norwalkfurniture.com
www.joeruggiero.com

Fine Pottery
Abigails
800-678-8485

Garden Accessories
Campo De'Fiori
413-528-9180

Area Rugs
Couristan
800-223-6186

Lamps & Chandeliers
Curry & Company, Inc.
404-885-1444

Wall Décor and Mirrors
Fine Art, Inc.
800-723-0348

Decorative Accessories
Original Book Works
401-885-0177

Novica.com
310-479-6685

Tansu Design Imports
415-255-2204

Decorative Wool Throws
M.A.N.E Enterprises
212-679-4640

Permanent Florals
New Growth Designs
252-752-6195

Textiles
Sunbrella
336-227-6211 x 1130

Decorative Trellis
Accents of France
323-653-4006

Pages 102-113

Furniture
Bassett Furniture
276-629-6000
www.bassettfurniture.com

Pages 114-125

Furniture
Habersham Furniture
1-800-HABERSHAM
www.habershamdesigns.com

Acknowledgments

I would like to especially thank my multi-talented assistant, Sandy Bowles, for her tireless efforts in coordinating the photography and copy materials for this book. Her creative input made this truly a collaborative effort.

I owe thanks as well to Kerry Glaser, of Concept Marketing Group, a New York licensing agency, for his invaluable insights into the world of designer collections.

Secret trade

Much credit for the inspiration for Celebrity Designer Collections goes to my wife, Hodges, an avid gardener and decorator. She provided a feminine perspective that "softened" my tendency toward the use of industry jargon. Each of The Perfect Home books contains a photograph I took of flowers from Hodges' garden.

Joe Carroll

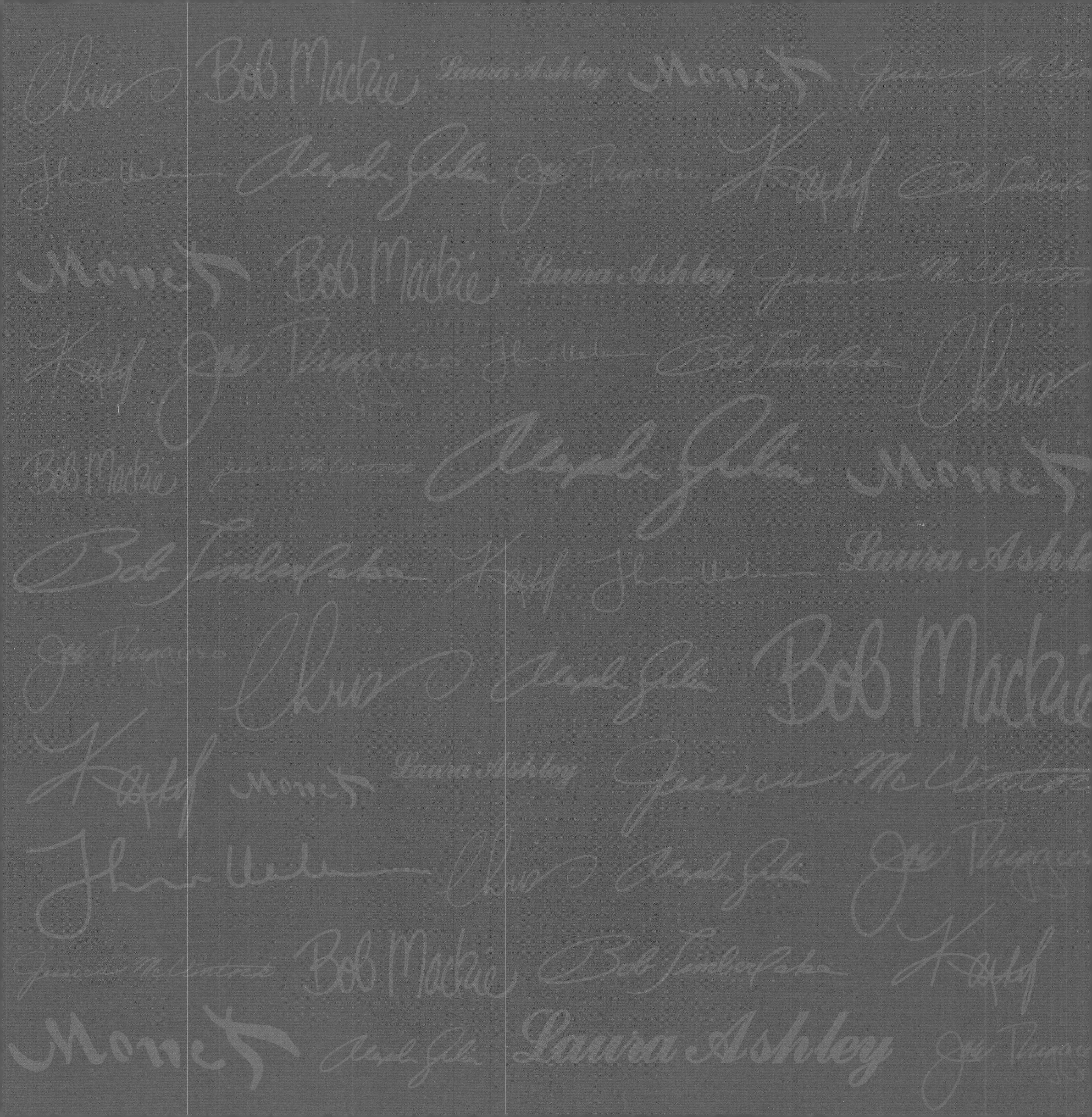
Bob Mackie
Laura Ashley
Monet